THE COLOUR OF LIFE

LECTOR HOUSE PUBLIC DOMAIN WORKS

THE COLOUR OF LIFE

ALICE MEYNELL

ISBN: 978-93-5614-287-9

Published: 1896

LECTOR HOUSE LLP
E-MAIL: lectorpublishing@gmail.com

THE COLOUR OF LIFE

AND OTHER ESSAYS
ON THINGS SEEN AND HEARD

BY

ALICE MEYNELL

1896

DEDICATED
TO
COVENTRY PATMORE

CONTENTS

THE COLOUR OF LIFE

Red has been praised for its nobility as the colour of life. But the true colour of life is not red. Red is the colour of violence, or of life broken open, edited, and published. Or if red is indeed the colour of life, it is so only on condition that it is not seen. Once fully visible, red is the colour of life violated, and in the act of betrayal and of waste. Red is the secret of life, and not the manifestation thereof. It is one of the things the value of which is secrecy, one of the talents that are to be hidden in a napkin. The true colour of life is the colour of the body, the colour of the covered red, the implicit and not explicit red of the living heart and the pulses. It is the modest colour of the unpublished blood.

So bright, so light, so soft, so mingled, the gentle colour of life is outdone by all the colours of the world. Its very beauty is that it is white, but less white than milk; brown, but less brown than earth; red, but less red than sunset or dawn. It is lucid, but less lucid than the colour of lilies. It has the hint of gold that is in all fine colour; but in our latitudes the hint is almost elusive. Under Sicilian skies, indeed, it is deeper than old ivory; but under the misty blue of the English zenith, and the warm grey of the London horizon, it is as delicately flushed as the paler wild roses, out to their utmost, flat as stars, in the hedges of the end of June.

For months together London does not see the colour of life in any mass. The human face does not give much of it, what with features, and beards, and the shadow of the top-hat and *chapeau melon* of man, and of the veils of woman. Besides, the colour of the face is subject to a thousand injuries and accidents. The popular face of the Londoner has soon lost its gold, its white, and the delicacy of its red and brown. We miss little beauty by the fact that it is never seen freely in great numbers out-of-doors. You get it in some quantity when all the heads of a great indoor meeting are turned at once upon a speaker; but it is only in the open air, needless to say, that the colour of life is in perfection, in the open air, "clothed with the sun," whether the sunshine be golden and direct, or dazzlingly diffused in grey.

The little figure of the London boy it is that has restored to the landscape the human colour of life. He is allowed to come out of all his ignominies, and to take the late colour of the midsummer north-west evening, on the borders of the Serpentine. At the stroke of eight he sheds the slough of nameless colours—all allied to the hues of dust, soot, and fog, which are the colours the world has chosen for its boys—and he makes, in his hundreds, a bright and delicate flush between the grey-blue water and the grey-blue sky. Clothed now with the sun, he is crowned by-and-by with twelve stars as he goes to bathe, and the reflection of an early moon is under his feet.

So little stands between a gamin and all the dignities of Nature. They are so quickly restored. There seems to be nothing to do, but only a little thing to undo. It is like the art of Eleonora Duse. The last and most finished action of her intellect, passion, and knowledge is, as it were, the flicking away of some insignificant thing mistaken for art by other actors, some little obstacle to the way and liberty of Nature.

All the squalor is gone in a moment, kicked off with the second boot, and the child goes shouting to complete the landscape with the lacking colour of life. You are inclined to wonder that, even undressed, he still shouts with a Cockney accent. You half expect pure vowels and elastic syllables from his restoration, his spring, his slenderness, his brightness, and his glow. Old ivory and wild rose in the deepening midsummer sun, he gives his colours to his world again.

It is easy to replace man, and it will take no great time, where Nature has lapsed, to replace Nature. It is always to do, by the happily easy way of doing nothing. The grass is always ready to grow in the streets—and no streets could ask for a more charming finish than your green grass. The gasometer even must fall to pieces unless it is renewed; but the grass renews itself. There is nothing so remediable as the work of modern man—"a thought which is also," as Mr Pecksniff said, "very soothing." And by remediable I mean, of course, destructible. As the bathing child shuffles off his garments—they are few, and one brace suffices him—so the land might always, in reasonable time, shuffle off its yellow brick and purple slate, and all the things that collect about railway stations. A single night almost clears the air of London.

But if the colour of life looks so well in the rather sham scenery of Hyde Park, it looks brilliant and grave indeed on a real sea-coast. To have once seen it there should be enough to make a colourist. O memorable little picture! The sun was gaining colour as it neared setting, and it set not over the sea, but over the land. The sea had the dark and rather stern, but not cold, blue of that aspect—the dark and not the opal tints. The sky was also deep. Everything was very definite, without mystery, and exceedingly simple. The most luminous thing was the shining white of an edge of foam, which did not cease to be white because it was a little golden and a little rosy in the sunshine. It was still the whitest thing imaginable. And the next most luminous thing was the little child, also invested with the sun and the colour of life.

In the case of women, it is of the living and unpublished blood that the violent world has professed to be delicate and ashamed. See the curious history of the political rights of woman under the Revolution. On the scaffold she enjoyed an ungrudged share in the fortunes of party. Political life might be denied her, but that seems a trifle when you consider how generously she was permitted political death. She was to spin and cook for her citizen in the obscurity of her living hours; but to the hour of her death was granted a part in the largest interests, social, national, international. The blood wherewith she should, according to Robespierre, have blushed to be seen or heard in the tribune, was exposed in the public sight unsheltered by her veins.

Against this there was no modesty. Of all privacies, the last and the inner-most—the privacy of death—was never allowed to put obstacles in the way of public action for a public cause. Women might be, and were, duly suppressed when, by the mouth of Olympe de Gouges, they claimed a "right to concur in the choice of representatives for the formation of the laws"; but in her person, too, they were liberally allowed to bear political responsibility to the Republic. Olympe de Gouges was guillotined. Robespierre thus made her public and complete amends.

A POINT OF BIOGRAPHY

There is hardly a writer now—of the third class probably not one—who has not something sharp and sad to say about the cruelty of Nature; not one who is able to attempt May in the woods without a modern reference to the manifold death and destruction with which the air, the branches, the mosses are said to be full.

But no one has paused in the course of these phrases to take notice of the curious and conspicuous fact of the suppression of death and of the dead throughout this landscape of manifest life. Where are they—all the dying, all the dead, of the populous woods? Where do they hide their little last hours, where are they buried? Where is the violence concealed? Under what gay custom and decent habit? You may see, it is true, an earth-worm in a robin's beak, and may hear a thrush breaking a snail's shell; but these little things are, as it were, passed by with a kind of twinkle for apology, as by a well-bred man who does openly some little solecism which is too slight for direct mention, and which a meaner man might hide or avoid. Unless you are very modern indeed, you twinkle back at the bird.

But otherwise there is nothing visible of the havoc and the prey and plunder. It is certain that much of the visible life passes violently into other forms, flashes without pause into another flame; but not all. Amid all the killing there must be much dying. There are, for instance, few birds of prey left in our more accessible counties now, and many thousands of birds must die uncaught by a hawk and unpierced. But if their killing is done so modestly, so then is their dying also. Short lives have all these wild things, but there are innumerable flocks of them always alive; they must die, then, in innumerable flocks. And yet they keep the millions of the dead out of sight.

Now and then, indeed, they may be betrayed. It happened in a cold winter. The late frosts were so sudden, and the famine was so complete, that the birds were taken unawares. The sky and the earth conspired that February to make known all the secrets; everything was published. Death was manifest. Editors, when a great man dies, are not more resolute than was the frost of '95.

The birds were obliged to die in public. They were surprised and forced to do thus. They became like Shelley in the monument which the art and imagination of England combined to raise to his memory at Oxford.

Frost was surely at work in both cases, and in both it wrought wrong. There is a similarity of unreason in betraying the death of a bird and in exhibiting the death of Shelley. The death of a soldier—*passe encore*. But the death of Shelley was not his goal. And the death of the birds is so little characteristic of them that, as has just been said, no one in the world is aware of their dying, except only in the case of birds in cages, who, again, are compelled to die with observation. The woodland is guarded and kept by a rule. There is no display of the battlefield in the fields. There is no tale of the game-bag, no boast. The hunting goes on, but with strange decorum. You may pass a fine season under the trees, and see nothing dead except here and there where a boy has been by, or a man with a trap, or a man with a gun. There is nothing like a butcher's shop in the woods.

But the biographers have always had other ways than those of the wild world. They will not have a man to die out of sight. I have turned over scores of "Lives," not to read them, but to see whether now and again there might be a "Life" which was not more emphatically a death. But there never is a modern biography that has taken the hint of Nature. One and all, these books have the disproportionate illness, the death out of all scale.

Even more wanton than the disclosure of a death is that of a mortal illness. If the man had recovered, his illness would have been rightly his own secret. But because he did not recover, it is assumed to be news for the first comer. Which of us would suffer the details of any physical suffering, over and done in our own lives, to be displayed and described? This is not a confidence we have a mind to make; and no one is authorised to ask for attention or pity on our behalf. The story of pain ought not to be told of us, seeing that by us it would assuredly not be told.

There is only one other thing that concerns a man still more exclusively, and that is his own mental illness, or the dreams and illusions of a long delirium. When he is in common language not himself, amends should be made for so bitter a paradox; he should be allowed such solitude as is possible to the alienated spirit; he should be left to the "not himself," and spared the intrusion against which he can so ill guard that he could hardly have even resented it.

The double helplessness of delusion and death should keep the door of Rossetti's house, for example, and refuse him to the reader. His mortal illness had nothing to do with his poetry. Some rather affected objection is taken every now and then to the publication of some facts (others being already well known) in the life of Shelley. Nevertheless, these are all, properly speaking, biography. What is not biography is the detail of the accident of the manner of his death, the detail of his cremation. Or if it was to be told—told briefly—it was certainly not for marble. Shelley's death had no significance, except inasmuch as he died young. It was a detachable and disconnected incident. Ah, that was a frost of fancy and of the heart that used it so, dealing with an insignificant fact, and conferring a futile immortality. Those are ill-named biographers who seem to think that a betrayal of the ways of death is a part of their ordinary duty, and that if material enough for a last chapter does not lie to their hand they are to search it out. They, of all survivors, are called upon, in honour and reason, to look upon a death with more composure. To those who loved the dead closely, this is, for a time, impossible. To them death becomes, for a year, disproportionate. Their dreams are fixed upon it night by night. They have, in those dreams, to find the dead in some labyrinth; they have to mourn his dying and to welcome his recovery in such a mingling of distress and of always incredulous happiness as is not known even to dreams save in that first year of separation. But they are not biographers.

If death is the privacy of the woods, it is the more conspicuously secret because it is their only privacy. You may watch or may surprise everything else. The nest is retired, not hidden. The chase goes on everywhere. It is wonderful how the perpetual chase seems to cause no perpetual fear. The songs are all audible. Life is undefended, careless, nimble and noisy.

It is a happy thing that minor artists have ceased, or almost ceased, to paint dead birds. Time was when they did it continually in that British School of water-colour art, stippled, of which surrounding nations, it was agreed, were envious. They must have killed their bird to paint him, for he is not to be caught dead. A bird is more easily caught alive than dead.

A poet, on the contrary, is easily—too easily—caught dead. Minor artists now seldom stipple the bird on its back, but a good sculptor and a University together modelled their Shelley on his back, unessentially drowned; and everybody may read about the sick mind of Dante Rossetti.

CLOUD

During a part of the year London does not see the clouds. Not to see the clear sky might seem her chief loss, but that is shared by the rest of England, and is, besides, but a slight privation. Not to see the clear sky is, elsewhere, to see the cloud. But not so in London. You may go for a week or two at a time, even though you hold your head up as you walk, and even though you have windows that really open, and yet you shall see no cloud, or but a single edge, the fragment of a form.

Guillotine windows never wholly open, but are filled with a doubled glass towards the sky when you open them towards the street. They are, therefore, a sure sign that for all the years when no other windows were used in London, nobody there cared much for the sky, or even knew so much as whether there were a sky.

But the privation of cloud is indeed a graver loss than the world knows. Terrestrial scenery is much, but it is not all. Men go in search of it; but the celestial scenery journeys to them. It goes its way round the world. It has no nation, it costs no weariness, it knows no bonds. The terrestrial scenery—the tourist's—is a prisoner compared with this. The tourist's scenery moves indeed, but only like Wordsworth's maiden, with earth's diurnal course; it is made as fast as its own graves. And for its changes it depends upon the mobility of the skies. The mere green flushing of its own sap makes only the least of its varieties; for the greater it must wait upon the visits of the light. Spring and autumn are inconsiderable events in a landscape compared with the shadows of a cloud.

The cloud controls the light, and the mountains on earth appear or fade according to its passage; they wear so simply, from head to foot, the luminous grey or the emphatic purple, as the cloud permits, that their own local colour and their own local season are lost and cease, effaced before the all-important mood of the cloud.

The sea has no mood except that of the sky and of its winds. It is the cloud that, holding the sun's rays in a sheaf as a giant holds a handful of spears, strikes the horizon, touches the extreme edge with a delicate revelation of light, or suddenly puts it out and makes the foreground shine.

Every one knows the manifest work of the cloud when it descends and partakes in the landscape obviously, lies half-way across the mountain slope, stoops to rain heavily upon the lake, and blots out part of the view by the rough method of standing in front of it. But its greatest things are done from its own place, aloft. Thence does it distribute the sun.

Thence does it lock away between the hills and valleys more mysteries than a poet conceals, but, like him, not by interception. Thence it writes out and cancels all the tracery of Monte Rosa, or lets the pencils of the sun renew them. Thence, hiding nothing, and yet making dark, it sheds deep colour upon the forest land of Sussex, so that, seen from the hills, all the country is divided between grave blue and graver sunlight.

And all this is but its influence, its secondary work upon the world. Its own beauty is unaltered when it has no earthly beauty to improve. It is always great: above the street, above the suburbs, above the gas-works and the stucco, above the faces of painted white houses—the painted surfaces that have been devised as the only things able to vulgarise light, as they catch it and reflect it grotesquely from their importunate gloss. This is to be well seen on a sunny evening in Regent Street.

Even here the cloud is not so victorious as when it towers above some little landscape of rather paltry interest—a conventional river heavy with water, gardens with their little evergreens, walks, and shrubberies; and thick trees impervious to the light, touched, as the novelists always have it, with "autumn tints." High over these rises, in the enormous scale of the scenery of clouds, what no man expected—an heroic sky. Few of the things that were ever done upon earth are great enough to be done under such a heaven. It was surely designed for other days. It is for an epic world. Your eyes sweep a thousand miles of cloud. What are the distances of earth to these, and what are the distances of the clear and cloudless sky? The very horizons of the landscape are near, for the round world dips so soon; and the distances of the mere clear sky are unmeasured—you rest upon nothing until you come to a star, and the star itself is immeasurable.

But in the sky of "sunny Alps" of clouds the sight goes farther, with conscious flight, than it could ever have journeyed otherwise. Man would not have known distance veritably without the clouds. There are mountains indeed, precipices and deeps, to which those of the earth are pigmy. Yet the sky-heights, being so far off, are not overpowering by disproportion, like some futile building fatuously made too big for the human measure. The cloud in its majestic place composes with a little Perugino tree. For you stand or stray in the futile building, while the cloud is no mansion for man, and out of reach of his limitations.

The cloud, moreover, controls the sun, not merely by keeping the custody of his rays, but by becoming the counsellor of his temper. The cloud veils an angry sun, or, more terribly, lets fly an angry ray, suddenly bright upon tree and tower, with iron-grey storm for a background. Or when anger had but threatened, the cloud reveals him, gentle beyond hope. It makes peace, constantly, just before sunset.

It is in the confidence of the winds, and wears their colours. There is a heavenly game, on south-west wind days, when the clouds are bowled by a breeze from behind the evening. They are round and brilliant, and come leaping up from the horizon for hours. This is a frolic and haphazard sky.

All unlike this is the sky that has a centre, and stands composed about it. As the clouds marshalled the earthly mountains, so the clouds in turn are now ranged. The tops of all the celestial Andes aloft are swept at once by a single ray, warmed with a single colour. Promontory after league-long promontory of a stiller Mediterranean in the sky is called out of mist and grey by the same finger. The cloudland is very great, but a sunbeam makes all its nations and continents sudden with light.

All this is for the untravelled. All the winds bring him this scenery. It is only in London, for part of the autumn and part of the winter, that the unnatural smoke-fog comes between. And for many and many a day no London eye can see the horizon, or the first threat of the cloud like a man's hand. There never was a great painter who had not exquisite horizons, and if Corot and Crome were right, the Londoner loses a great thing.

He loses the coming of the cloud, and when it is high in air he loses its shape. A cloud-lover is not content to see a snowy and rosy head piling into the top of the heavens; he wants to see the base and the altitude. The perspective of a cloud is a great part of its design—whether it lies so that you can look along the immense horizontal distances of its floor, or whether it rears so upright a pillar that you look up its mountain steeps in the sky as you look at the rising heights of a mountain that stands, with you, on the earth.

The cloud has a name suggesting darkness; nevertheless, it is not merely the guardian of the sun's rays and their director. It is the sun's treasurer; it holds the light that the world has lost. We talk of sunshine and moonshine, but not of cloud-shine, which is yet one of the illuminations of our skies. A shining cloud is one of the most majestic of all secondary lights. If the reflecting moon is the bride, this is the friend of the bridegroom.

Needless to say, the cloud of a thunderous summer is the most beautiful of all. It has spaces of a grey for which there is no name, and no other cloud looks over at a vanishing sun from such heights of blue air. The shower-cloud, too, with its thin edges, comes across the sky with so influential a flight that no ship going out to sea can be better worth watching. The dullest thing perhaps in the London streets is that people take their rain there without knowing anything of the cloud that drops it. It is merely rain, and means wetness. The shower-cloud there has limits of time, but no limits of form, and no history whatever. It has not come from the clear edge of the plain to the south, and will not shoulder anon the hill to the north. The rain, for this city, hardly comes or goes; it does but begin and stop. No one looks after it on the path of its retreat.

WINDS OF THE WORLD

Every wind is, or ought to be, a poet; but one is classic and converts everything in his day co-unity; another is a modern man, whose words clothe his thoughts, as the modern critics used to say prettily in the early sixties, and therefore are separable. This wind, again, has a style, and that wind a mere manner. Nay, there are breezes from the east-south-east, for example, that have hardly even a manner. You can hardly name them unless you look at the weather vane. So they do not convince you by voice or colour of breath; you place their origin and assign them a history according as the hesitating arrow points on the top of yonder ill-designed London spire.

The most certain and most conquering of all is the south-west wind. You do not look to the weather-vane to decide what shall be the style of your greeting to his morning. There is no arbitrary rule of courtesy between you and him, and you need no arrow to point to his distinctions, and to indicate to you the right manner of treating such a visitant.

He prepares the dawn. While it is still dark the air is warned of his presence, and before the window was opened he was already in the room. His sun—for the sun is his—rises in a south-west mood, with a bloom on the blue, the grey, or the gold. When the south-west is cold, the cold is his own cold—round, blunt, full, and gradual in its very strength. It is a fresh cold, that comes with an approach, and does not challenge you in the manner of an unauthorised stranger, but instantly gets your leave, and even a welcome to your house of life. He follows your breath in at your throat, and your eyes are open to let him in, even when he is cold. Your blood cools, but does not hide from him.

He has a splendid way with his sky. In his flight, which is that, not of a bird, but of a flock of birds, he flies high and low at once: high with his higher clouds, that keep long in the sight of man, seeming to move slowly; and low with the coloured clouds that breast the hills and are near to the tree-tops. These the south-west wind tosses up from his soft horizon, round and successive. They are tinted somewhat like ripe clover-fields, or like hay-fields just before the cutting, when all the grass is in flower, and they are, oftener than all other clouds, in shadow. These low-lying flocks are swift and brief; the wind casts them before him, from the western verge to the eastern.

Corot has painted so many south-west winds that one might question whether he ever painted, in his later manner at least, any others. His skies are thus in the act of flight, with lower clouds outrunning the higher, the farther vapours moving like a fleet out at sea, and the nearer like dolphins. In his "Classical Landscape: Italy," the master has indeed for once a sky that seems at anchor, or at least that moves with "no pace perceived." The vibrating wings are folded, and Corot's wind, that flew through so many springs, summers, and Septembers for him (he was seldom a painter of very late autumn), that was mingled with so many aspen-leaves, that strewed his forests with wood for the gatherer, and blew the broken lights into the glades, is charmed into stillness, and the sky into another kind of immortality. Nor are the trees in this antique landscape the trees so long intimate with Corot's south-west wind, so often entangled with his uncertain twilights. They are as quiet as the cloud, and such as the long and wild breezes of Romance have never shaken or enlaced.

Upon all our islands this south-west wind is the sea wind. But elsewhere there are sea winds that are not from the south-west. They, too, none the less, are conquerors. They, too, are always strong, compelling winds that take possession of the light, the shadow, the sun, moon, and stars, and constrain them all alike to feel the sea. Not a field, not a hillside, on a sea-wind day, but shines with some soft sea-lights. The moon's little boat tosses on a sea-wind night.

The south-west wind takes the high Italian coasts. He gathers the ilex woods together and throngs them close, as a sheep-dog gathers the sheep. They crowd for shelter, and a great wall, leaning inland also, with its strong base to the sea, receives them. It is blank and sunny, and the trees within are sunny and dark, serried, and their tops swept and flattened by months of sea-storms. On the farther side there are gardens—gardens that have in their midst those quietest things in all the world and most windless, box-hedges and ponds. The gardens take shelter behind the scared and hurried ilex woods, and the sea-wind spares them and breaks upon the mountain. But the garden also is his, and his wild warm days have filled it with orange-trees and roses, and have given all the abundant charm to its gay neglect, to its grass-grown terraces, and to all its lapsed, forsaken, and forgotten dainties.

Nothing of the nature in this seaward Italy would be so beautiful without the touch of man and of the sea gales.

When the south-west wind brings his rain he brings it with the majestic onset announced by his breath. And when the light follows, it comes from his own doorway in the verge. His are the opened evenings after a day shut down with cloud. He fills the air with innumerable particles of moisture that scatter and bestow the sun. There are no other days like his, of so universal a harmony, so generous.

The north wind has his own landscape, too; but the east wind never. The aspect which he gives to the day is not all his own. The sunshine is sweet in spite of him. The clouds go under his whip, but they have kinder greys than should be the colours of his cold. Not on an east-wind day are these races in heaven, for the clouds are all far off. His rain is angry, and it flies against the sunset. The world is not one in his reign, but rather there is a perpetual revolt or difference. The lights and shadows are not all his. The waxing and waning hours are disaffected. He has not a great style, and does not convince the day.

All the four winds are brave, and not the less brave because, on their way through town, they are betrayed for a moment into taking part in any paltriness that may be there. On their way from the Steppes to the Atlantic they play havoc with the nerves of very insignificant people. A part, as it were, of every gale that starts in the far north-east finds its goal in the breath of a reluctant citizen.

You will meet a wind of the world nimble and eager in a sorry street. But these are only accidents of the way — the winds go free again. Those that do not go free, but close their course, are those that are breathed by the nostrils of living creatures. A great flock of those wild birds come to a final pause in London, and fan the fires of life with those wings in the act of folding. In the blood and breath of a child close the influences of continent and sea.

THE HONOURS OF MORTALITY

The brilliant talent which has quite lately and quite suddenly arisen, to devote itself to the use of the day or of the week, in illustrated papers—the enormous production of art in black and white—is assuredly a confession that the Honours of Mortality are worth working for. Fifty years ago, men worked for the honours of immortality; these were the commonplace of their ambition; they declined to attend to the beauty of things of use that were destined to be broken and worn out, and they looked forward to surviving themselves by painting bad pictures; so that what to do with their bad pictures in addition to our own has become the problem of the nation and of the householder alike. To-day men have began to learn that their sons will be grateful to them for few bequests. Art consents at last to work upon the tissue and the china that are doomed to the natural and necessary end—destruction; and art shows a most dignified alacrity to do her best, daily, for the "process," and for oblivion.

Doubtless this abandonment of hopes so large at once and so cheap costs the artist something; nay, it implies an acceptance of the inevitable that is not less than heroic. And the reward has been in the singular and manifest increase of vitality in this work which is done for so short a life. Fittingly indeed does life reward the acceptance of death, inasmuch as to die is to have been alive. There is a real circulation of blood-quick use, brief beauty, abolition, recreation. The honour of the day is for ever the honour of that day. It goes into the treasury of things that are honestly and—completely ended and done with. And when can so happy a thing be said of a lifeless oil-painting? Who of the wise would hesitate? To be honourable for one day—one named and dated day, separate from all other days of the ages—or to be for an unlimited time tedious?

AT MONASTERY GATES

No woman has ever crossed the inner threshold, or shall ever cross it, unless a queen, English or foreign, should claim her privilege. Therefore, if a woman records here the slighter things visible of the monastic life, it is only because she was not admitted to see more than beautiful courtesy and friendliness were able to show her in guest-house and garden.

The Monastery is of fresh-looking Gothic, by Pugin—the first of the dynasty: it is reached by the white roads of a limestone country, and backed by a young plantation, and it gathers its group of buildings in a cleft high up among the hills of Wales. The brown habit is this, and these are the sandals, that come and go by hills of finer, sharper, and loftier line, edging the dusk and dawn of an Umbrian sky. Just such a Via Crucis climbs the height above Orta, and from the foot of its final crucifix you can see the sunrise touch the top of Monte Rosa, while the encircled lake below is cool with the last of the night. The same order of friars keep that sub-Alpine Monte Sacro, and the same have set the Kreuzberg beyond Bonn with the same steep path by the same fourteen chapels, facing the Seven Mountains and the Rhine.

Here, in North Wales, remote as the country is, with the wheat green over the blunt hill-tops, and the sky vibrating with larks, a long wing of smoke lies round the horizon. The country, rather thinly and languidly cultivated above, has a valuable sub-soil, and is burrowed with mines; the breath of pit and factory, out of sight, thickens the lower sky, and lies heavily over the sands of Dee. It leaves the upper blue clear and the head of Orion, but dims the flicker of Sirius and shortens the steady ray of the evening star. The people scattered about are not mining people, but half-hearted agriculturists, and very poor. Their cottages are rather cabins; not a tiled roof is in the country, but the slates have taken some beauty with time, having dips and dimples, and grass upon their edges. The walls are all thickly whitewashed, which is a pleasure to see. How willingly would one swish the harmless whitewash over more than half the colour—over all the chocolate and all the blue—with which the buildings of the world are stained! You could not wish for a better, simpler, or fresher harmony than whitewash makes with the slight sunshine and the bright grey of an English sky.

The grey-stone, grey-roofed monastery looks young in one sense—it is modern; and the friars look young in another—they are like their brothers of an earlier time. No one, except the journalists of yesterday, would spend upon them those tedious words, "quaint," or "old world." No such weary adjectives are spoken here, unless it be by the excursionists.

With large aprons tied over their brown habits, the Lay Brothers work upon their land, planting parsnips in rows, or tending a prosperous bee-farm. A young friar, who sang the High Mass yesterday, is gaily hanging the washed linen in the sun. A printing press, and a machine which slices turnips, are at work in an outhouse, and the yard thereby is guarded by a St Bernard, whose single evil deed was that under one of the obscure impulses of a dog's heart—atoned for by long and self-conscious remorse—he bit the poet; and tried, says one of the friars, to make doggerel of him. The poet, too, lives at the monastery gates, and on monastery ground, in a seclusion which the tidings of the sequence of his editions hardly reaches. There is no disturbing renown to be got among the cabins of the Flintshire hills. Homeward, over the verge, from other valleys, his light figure flits at nightfall, like a moth.

To the coming and going of the friars, too, the village people have become well used, and the infrequent excursionists, for lack of intelligence and of any knowledge that would refer to history, look at them without obtrusive curiosity. It was only from a Salvation Army girl that you heard the brutal word of contempt. She had come to the place with some companions, and with them was trespassing, as she was welcome to do, within the monastery grounds. She stood, a figure for Bournemouth pier, in her grotesque bonnet, and watched the son of the Umbrian saint—the friar who walks among the Giotto frescoes at Assisi and between the cypresses of Bello Sguardo, and has paced the centuries continually since the coming of the friars. One might have asked of her the kindness of a fellow-feeling. She and he alike were so habited as to show the world that their life was aloof from its "idle business." By some such phrase, at least, the friar would assuredly have attempted to include her in any spiritual honours ascribed to him. Or one might have asked of her the condescension of forbearance. "Only fancy," said the Salvation Army girl, watching the friar out of sight, "only fancy making such a fool of one's self!"

The great hood of the friars, which is drawn over the head in Zurbaran's ecstatic picture, is turned to use when the friars are busy. As a pocket it relieves the over-burdened hands. A bottle of the local white wine made by the brotherhood at Genoa, and sent to this house by the West, is carried in the cowl as a present to the stranger at the gates. The friars tell how a brother resolved, at Shrovetide, to make pancakes, and not only to make, but also to toss them. Those who chanced to be in the room stood prudently aside, and the brother tossed boldly. But that was the last that was seen of his handiwork. Victor Hugo sings in *La Légende des Siècles* of disappearance as the thing which no creature is able to achieve: here the impossibility seemed to be accomplished by quite an ordinary and a simple pancake. It was clean gone, and there was an end of it. Nor could any explanation of this ceasing of a pancake from the midst of the visible world be so much as divined by the spectators. It was only when the brother, in church, knelt down to meditate and drew his cowl about his head that the accident was explained.

Every midnight the sweet contralto bells call the community, who get up gaily to this difficult service. Of all duties this one never grows easy or familiar, and therefore never habitual. It is something to have found but one act aloof from habit. It is not merely that the friars overcome the habit of sleep. The subtler point is that they can never acquire the habit of sacrificing sleep. What art, what literature, or what life but would gain a secret security by such a point of perpetual freshness and perpetual initiative? It is not possible to get up at midnight without a will that is new night by night. So should the writer's work be done, and, with an intention perpetually unique, the poet's.

The contralto bells have taught these Western hills the "Angelus" of the French fields, and the hour of night—*l'ora di notte*—which rings with so melancholy a note from the village belfries on the Adriatic littoral, when the latest light is passing. It is the prayer for the dead: "Out of the depths have I cried unto Thee, O Lord."

The little flocks of novices, on paschal evenings, are folded to the sound of that evening prayer. The care of them is the central work of the monastery, which is placed in so remote a country because it is principally a place of studies. So much elect intellect and strength of heart withdrawn from the traffic of the world! True, the friars are not doing the task which Carlyle set mankind as a refuge from despair. These "bearded counsellors of God" keep their cells, read, study, suffer, sing, hold silence; whereas they might be "operating"—beautiful word!—upon the Stock Exchange, or painting Academy pictures, or making speeches, or reluctantly jostling other men for places. They might be among the involuntary busybodies who are living by futile tasks the need whereof is a discouraged fiction. There is absolutely no limit to the superfluous activities, to the art, to the literature, implicitly renounced by the dwellers within such walls as these. The output—again a beautiful word—of the age is lessened by this abstention. None the less hopes the stranger and pilgrim to pause and knock once again upon those monastery gates.

RUSHES AND REEDS

Taller than the grass and lower than the trees, there is another growth that feels the implicit spring. It had been more abandoned to winter than even the short grass shuddering under a wave of east wind, more than the dumb trees. For the multitudes of sedges, rushes, canes, and reeds were the appropriate lyre of the cold. On them the nimble winds played their dry music. They were part of the winter. It looked through them and spoke through them. They were spears and javelins in array to the sound of the drums of the north.

The winter takes fuller possession of these things than of those that stand solid. The sedges whistle his tune. They let the colour of his light look through—low-flying arrows and bright bayonets of winter day.

The multitudes of all reeds and rushes grow out of bounds. They belong to the margins of lands, the space between the farms and the river, beyond the pastures, and where the marsh in flower becomes perilous footing for the cattle. They are the fringe of the low lands, the sign of streams. They grow tall between you and the near horizon of flat lands. They etch their sharp lines upon the sky; and near them grow flowers of stature, including the lofty yellow lily.

Our green country is the better for the grey, soft, cloudy darkness of the sedge, and our full landscape is the better for the distinction of its points, its needles, and its resolute right lines.

Ours is a summer full of voices, and therefore it does not so need the sound of rushes; but they are most sensitive to the stealthy breezes, and betray the passing of a wind that even the tree-tops knew not of. Sometimes it is a breeze unfelt, but the stiff sedges whisper it along a mile of marsh. To the strong wind they bend, showing the silver of their sombre little tassels as fish show the silver of their sides turning in the pathless sea. They are unanimous. A field of tall flowers tosses many ways in one warm gale, like the many lovers of a poet who have a thousand reasons for their love; but the rushes, more strongly tethered, are swept into a single attitude, again and again, at every renewal of the storm.

Between the pasture and the wave, the many miles of rushes and reeds in England seem to escape that insistent ownership which has so changed (except for a few forests and downs) the aspect of England, and has in fact made the landscape. Cultivation makes the landscape elsewhere, rather than ownership, for the boundaries in the south are not conspicuous; but here it is ownership. But the rushes are a gipsy people, amongst us, yet out of reach. The landowner, if he is rather a gross man, believes these races of reeds are his. But if he is a man of sensibility, depend upon it he has his interior doubts. His property, he says, goes right down to the centre of the earth, in the shape of a wedge; how high up it goes into the air it would be difficult to say, and obviously the shape of the wedge must be continued in the direction of increase. We may therefore proclaim his right to the clouds and their cargo. It is true that as his ground game is apt to go upon his neighbour's land to be shot, so the clouds may now and then spend his showers elsewhere. But the great thing is the view. A well-appointed country-house sees nothing out of the windows that is not its own. But he who tells you so, and proves it to you by his own view, is certainly disturbed by an unspoken doubt, if his otherwise contented eyes should happen to be caught by a region of rushes. The water is his—he had the pond made; or the river, for a space, and the fish, for a time. But the bulrushes, the reeds! One wonders whether a very thorough landowner, but a sensitive one, ever resolved that he would endure this sort of thing no longer, and went out armed and had a long acre of sedges scythed to death.

They are probably outlaws. They are dwellers upon thresholds and upon margins, as the gipsies make a home upon the green edges of a road. No wild flowers, however wild, are rebels. The copses and their primroses are good subjects, the oaks are loyal. Now and then, though, one has a kind of suspicion of some of the other kinds of trees—the Corot trees. Standing at a distance from the more ornamental trees, from those of fuller foliage, and from all the indeciduous shrubs and the conifers (manifest property, every one), two or three translucent aspens, with which the very sun and the breath of earth are entangled, have sometimes seemed to wear a certain look—an extra-territorial look, let us call it. They are suspect. One is inclined to shake a doubtful head at them.

And the landowner feels it. He knows quite well, though he may not say so, that the Corot trees, though they do not dwell upon margins, are in spirit almost as extraterritorial as the rushes. In proof of this he very often cuts them down, out of the view, once for all. The view is better, as a view, without them. Though their roots are in his ground right enough, there is a something about their heads—. But the reason he gives for wishing them away is merely that they are "thin." A man does not always say everything.

ELEONORA DUSE

The Italian woman is very near to Nature; so is true drama.

Acting is not to be judged like some other of the arts, and praised for a "noble convention." Painting, indeed, is not praised amiss with that word; painting is obviously an art that exists by its convention—the convention is the art. But far otherwise is it with the art of acting, where there is no representative material; where, that is, the man is his own material, and there is nothing between. With the actor the style is the man, in another, a more immediate, and a more obvious sense than was ever intended by that saying. Therefore we may allow the critic—and not accuse him of reaction—to speak of the division between art and Nature in the painting of a landscape, but we cannot let him say the same things of acting. Acting has a technique, but no convention.

Once for all, then, to say that acting reaches the point of Nature, and touches it quick, is to say all. In other arts imitation is more or less fatuous, illusion more or less vulgar. But acting is, at its less good, imitation; at its best, illusion; at its worst, and when it ceases to be an art, convention.

But the idea that acting is conventional has inevitably come about in England. For it is, in fact, obliged, with us, to defeat and destroy itself by taking a very full, entire, tedious, and impotent convention; a complete body of convention; a convention of demonstrativeness—of voice and manners intended to be expressive, and, in particular, a whole weak and unimpulsive convention of gesture. The English manners of real life are so negative and still as to present no visible or audible drama; and drama is for hearing and for vision. Therefore our acting (granting that we have any acting, which is granting much) has to create its little different and complementary world, and to make the division of "art" from Nature—the division which, in this one art, is fatal.

This is one simple and sufficient reason why we have no considerable acting; though we may have more or less interesting and energetic or graceful conventions that pass for art. But any student of international character knows well enough that there are also supplementary reasons of weight. For example, it is bad to make a conventional world of the stage, but it is doubly bad to make it badly—which, it must be granted, we do. When we are anything of the kind, we are intellectual rather than intelligent; whereas outward-streaming intelligence makes the actor. We are pre-occupied, and therefore never single, never wholly possessed by the one thing at a time; and so forth.

On the other hand, Italians are expressive. They are so possessed by the one thing at a time as never to be habitual in any lifeless sense. They have no habits to overcome by something arbitrary and intentional. Accordingly, you will find in the open-air theatre of many an Italian province, away from the high roads, an art of drama that our capital cannot show, so high is it, so fine, so simple, so complete, so direct, so momentary and impassioned, so full of singleness and of multitudinous impulses of passion.

Signora Duse is not different in kind from these unrenowned. What they are, she is in a greater degree. She goes yet further, and yet closer. She has an exceptionally large and liberal intelligence. If lesser actors give themselves entirely to the part, and to the large moment of the part, she, giving herself, has more to give.

Add to this nature of hers that she stages herself and her acting with singular knowledge and ease, and has her technique so thoroughly as to be able to forget it—for this is the one only thing that is the better for habit, and ought to be habitual. There is but one passage of her mere technique in which she fails so to slight it. It is in the long exchange of stove-side talk between Nora and the other woman of "The Doll's House." Signora Duse may have felt some misgivings as to the effect of a dialogue having so little symmetry, such half-hearted feeling, and, in a word, so little visible or audible drama as this. Needless to say, the misgiving is not apparent; what is too apparent is simply the technique. For instance, she shifts her position with evident system and notable skill. The whole conversation becomes a dance of change and counterchange of place.

Nowhere else does the perfect technical habit lapse, and nowhere at all does the habit of acting exist with her.

I have spoken of this actress's nationality and of her womanhood together. They are inseparable. Nature is the only authentic art of the stage, and the Italian woman is natural: none other so natural and so justified by her nature as Eleonora Duse; but all, as far as their nature goes, natural. Moreover, they are women freer than other Europeans from the minor vanities. Has any one yet fully understood how her liberty in this respect gives to the art of Signora Duse room and action? Her countrywomen have no anxious vanities, because, for one reason, they are generally "sculpturesque," and are very little altered by mere accidents of dress or arrangement. Such as they are, they are so once for all; whereas, the turn of a curl makes all the difference with women of less grave physique. Italians are not uneasy.

Signora Duse has this immunity, but she has a far nobler deliverance from vanities, in her own peculiar distance and dignity. She lets her beautiful voice speak, unwatched and unchecked, from the very life of the moment. It runs up into the high notes of indifference, or, higher still, into those of *ennui*, as in the earlier scenes of *Divorçons*; or it grows sweet as summer with joy, or cracks and breaks outright, out of all music, and out of all control. Passion breaks it so for her.

As for her inarticulate sounds, which are the more intimate and the truer words of her meaning, they, too, are Italian and natural. English women, for instance, do not make them. They are sounds *à bouche fermée*, at once private and irrepressible. They are not demonstrations intended for the ears of others; they are her own. Other actresses, even English, and even American, know how to make inarticulate cries, with open mouth; Signora Duse's noise is not a cry; it is her very thought audible—the thought of the woman she is playing, who does not at every moment give exact words to her thought, but does give it significant sound.

When *la femme de Claude* is trapped by the man who has come in search of the husband's secret, and when she is obliged to sit and listen to her own evil history as he tells it her, she does not interrupt the telling with the outcries that might be imagined by a lesser actress, she accompanies it. Her lips are close, but her throat is vocal. None who heard it can forget the speech-within-speech of one of these comprehensive noises. It was when the man spoke, for her further confusion, of the slavery to which she had reduced her lovers; she followed him, aloof, with a twang of triumph.

If Parisians say, as they do, that she makes a bad Parisienne, it is because she can be too nearly a woman untamed. They have accused her of lack of elegance— in that supper scene of *La Dame aux Camélias*, for instance; taking for ill-breeding, in her Marguerite, that which is Italian merely and simple. Whether, again, Cyprienne, in *Divorçons*, can at all be considered a lady may be a question; but this is quite unquestionable—that she is rather more a lady, and not less, when Signora Duse makes her a savage. But really the result is not at all Parisian.

It seems possible that the French sense does not well distinguish, and has no fine perception of that affinity with the peasant which remains with the great ladies of the old civilisation of Italy, and has so long disappeared from those of the younger civilisations of France and England—a paradox. The peasant's gravity, directness, and carelessness—a kind of uncouthness which is neither graceless nor, in any intolerable English sense, vulgar—are to be found in the unceremonious moments of every cisalpine woman, however elect her birth and select her conditions. In Italy the lady is not a creature described by negatives, as an author who is always right has defined the lady to be in England. Even in France she is not that, and between the Frenchwoman and the Italian there are the Alps. In a word, the educated Italian *mondaine* is, in the sense (also untranslatable) of singular, insular, and absolutely British usage, a Native. None the less would she be surprised to find herself accused of a lack of dignity.

As to intelligence—a little intelligence is sufficiently dramatic, if it is single. A child doing one thing at a time and doing it completely, produces to the eye a better impression of mental life than one receives from—well, from a lecturer.

DONKEY RACES

English acting had for some time past still been making a feint of running the race that wins. The retort, the interruption, the call, the reply, the surprise, had yet kept a spoilt tradition of suddenness and life. You had, indeed, to wait for an interruption in dialogue—it is true you had to wait for it; so had the interrupted speaker on the stage. But when the interruption came, it had still a false air of vivacity; and the waiting of the interrupted one was so ill done, with so roving an eye and such an arrest and failure of convention, such a confession of a blank, as to prove that there remained a kind of reluctant and inexpert sense of movement. It still seemed as though the actor and the actress acknowledged some forward tendency.

Not so now. The serious stage is openly the scene of the race that loses. The donkey race is candidly the model of the talk in every tragedy that has a chance of popular success. Who shall be last? The hands of the public are for him, or for her. A certain actress who has "come to the front of her profession" holds, for a time, the record of delay. "Come to the front," do they say? Surely the front of her profession must have moved in retreat, to gain upon her tardiness. It must have become the back of her profession before ever it came up with her.

It should rejoice those who enter for this kind of racing that the record need never finally be beaten. The possibilities of success are incalculable. The play has perforce to be finished in a night, it is true, but the minor characters, the subordinate actors, can be made to bear the burden of that necessity. The principals, or those who have come "to the front of their profession," have an almost unlimited opportunity and liberty of lagging.

Besides, the competitor in a donkey race is not, let it be borne in mind, limited to the practice of his own tediousness. Part of his victory is to be ascribed to his influence upon others. It may be that a determined actor—a man of more than common strength of will—may so cause his colleague to get on (let us say "get on," for everything in this world is relative); may so, then, compel the other actor, with whom he is in conversation, to get on, as to secure his own final triumph by indirect means as well as by direct. To be plain, for the sake of those unfamiliar with the sports of the village, the rider in a donkey race may, and does, cudgel the mounts of his rivals.

Consider, therefore, how encouraging the prospect really is. The individual actor may fail—in fact, he must. Where two people ride together on horseback, the married have ever been warned, one must ride behind. And when two people are speaking slowly one must needs be the slowest. Comparative success implies the comparative failure. But where this actor or that actress fails, the great cause of slowness profits, obviously. The record is advanced. Pshaw! the word "advanced" comes unadvised to the pen. It is difficult to remember in what a fatuous theatrical Royal Presence one is doing this criticism, and how one's words should go backwards, without exception, in homage to this symbol of a throne.

It is not long since there took place upon the principal stage in London the most important event in donkey-racing ever known until that first night. A tragedian and a secondary actor of renown had a duet together. It was in "The Dead Heart." No one who heard it can possibly have yet forgotten it. The two men used echoes of one another's voice, then outpaused each other. It was a contest so determined, so unrelaxed, so deadly, so inveterate that you might have slept between its encounters. You did sleep. These men were strong men, and knew what they wanted. It is tremendous to watch the struggle of such resolves. They had their purpose in their grasp, their teeth were set, their will was iron. They were foot to foot.

And next morning you saw by the papers that the secondary, but still renowned, actor, had succeeded in sharing the principal honours of the piece. So uncommonly well had he done, even for him. Then you understood that, though you had not known it, the tragedian must have been beaten in that dialogue. He had suffered himself in an instant of weakness, to be stimulated; he had for a moment—only a moment—got on.

That night was influential. We may see its results everywhere, and especially in Shakespeare. Our tragic stage was always—well, different, let us say—different from the tragic stage of Italy and France. It is now quite unlike, and frankly so. The spoilt tradition of vitality has been explicitly abandoned. The interrupted one waits, no longer with a roving eye, but with something almost of dignity, as though he were fulfilling ritual.

Benvolio and Mercutio outlag one another in hunting after the leaping Romeo. They call without the slightest impetus. One can imagine how the true Mercutio called—certainly not by rote. There must have been pauses indeed, brief and short-breath'd pauses of listening for an answer, between every nickname. But the nicknames were quick work. At the Lyceum they were quite an effort of memory: "Romeo! Humours! Madman! Passion! Lover!"

The actress of Juliet, speaking the words of haste, makes her audience wait to hear them. Nothing more incongruous than Juliet's harry of phrase and the actress's leisure of phrasing. None act, none speak, as though there were such a thing as impulse in a play. To drop behind is the only idea of arriving. The nurse ceases to be absurd, for there is no one readier with a reply than she. Or, rather, her delays are so altered by exaggeration as to lose touch with Nature. If it is ill enough to hear haste drawled out, it is ill, too, to hear slowness out-tarried. The true nurse of Shakespeare lags with her news because her ignorant wits are easily astray, as lightly caught as though they were light, which they are not; but the nurse of the stage is never simply astray: she knows beforehand how long she means to be, and never, never forgets what kind of race is the race she is riding. The Juliet of the stage seems to consider that there is plenty of time for her to discover which is slain—Tybalt or her husband; she is sure to know some time; it can wait.

A London success, when you know where it lies, is not difficult to achieve. Of all things that can be gained by men or women about their business, there is one thing that can be gained without fear of failure. This is time. To gain time requires so little wit that, except for competition, every one could be first at the game. In fact, time gains itself. The actor is really not called upon to do anything. There is nothing, accordingly, for which our actors and actresses do not rely upon time. For humour even, when the humour occurs in tragedy, they appeal to time. They give blanks to their audiences to be filled up.

It might be possible to have tragedies written from beginning to end for the service of the present kind of "art." But the tragedies we have are not so written. And being what they are, it is not vivacity that they lose by this length of pause, this length of phrasing, this illimitable tiresomeness; it is life itself. For the life of a scene conceived directly is its directness; the life of a scene created simply is its simplicity. And simplicity, directness, impetus, emotion, nature fall out of the trailing, loose, long dialogue, like fish from the loose meshes of a net—they fall out, they drift off, they are lost.

The universal slowness, moreover, is not good for metre. Even when an actress speaks her lines as lines, and does not drop into prose by slipping here and there a syllable, she spoils the *tempo* by inordinate length of pronunciation. Verse cannot keep upon the wing without a certain measure in the movement of the pinion. Verse is a flight.

GRASS

Now and then, at regular intervals of the summer, the Suburb springs for a time from its mediocrity; but an inattentive eye might not see why, or might not seize the cause of the bloom and of the new look of humility and dignity that makes the Road, the Rise, and the Villas seem suddenly gentle, gay and rather shy.

It is no change in the gardens. These are, as usual, full, abundant, fragrant, and quite uninteresting, keeping the traditional secret by which the suburban rose, magnolia, clematis, and all other flowers grow dull—not in colour, but in spirit—between the yellow brick house-front and the iron railings. Nor is there anything altered for the better in the houses themselves.

Nevertheless, the little, common, prosperous road, has bloomed, you cannot tell how. It is unexpectedly liberal, fresh, and innocent. The soft garden-winds that rustle its shrubs are, for the moment, genuine.

Another day and all is undone. The Rise is its daily self again—a road of flowers and foliage that is less pleasant than a fairly well-built street. And if you happen to find the men at work on the re-transformation, you become aware of the accident that made all this difference. It lay in the little border of wayside grass which a row of public servants—men with spades and a cart—are in the act of tidying up. Their way of tidying it up is to lay its little corpse all along the suburban roadside, and then to carry it away to some parochial dust-heap.

But for the vigilance of Vestries, grass would reconcile everything. When the first heat of the summer was over, a few nights of rain altered all the colour of the world. It had been the brown and russet of drought—very beautiful in landscape, but lifeless; it became a translucent, profound, and eager green. The citizen does not spend attention on it.

Why, then, is his vestry so alert, so apprehensive, so swift; in perception so instant, in execution so prompt, so silent in action, so punctual in destruction? The vestry keeps, as it were, a tryst with the grass. The "sunny spots of greenery" are given just time enough to grow and be conspicuous, and the barrow is there, true to time, and the spade. (To call that spade a spade hardly seems enough.)

For the gracious grass of the summer has not been content within enclosures. It has—or would have—cheered up and sweetened everything. Over asphalte it could not prevail, and it has prettily yielded to asphalte, taking leave to live and let live. It has taken the little strip of ground next to the asphalte, between this and the kerb, and again the refuse of ground between the kerb and the roadway. The man of business walking to the station with a bag could have his asphalte all unbroken, and the butcher's boy in his cart was not annoyed. The grass seemed to respect everybody's views, and to take only what nobody wanted. But these gay and lowly ways will not escape a vestry.

There is no wall so impregnable or so vulgar, but a summer's grass will attempt it. It will try to persuade the yellow brick, to win the purple slate, to reconcile stucco. Outside the authority of the suburbs it has put a luminous touch everywhere. The thatch of cottages has given it an opportunity. It has perched and alighted in showers and flocks. It has crept and crawled, and stolen its hour. It has made haste between the ruts of cart wheels, so they were not too frequent. It has been stealthy in a good cause, and bold out of reach. It has been the most defiant runaway, and the meekest lingerer. It has been universal, ready and potential in every place, so that the happy country—village and field alike—has been all grass, with mere exceptions.

And all this the grass does in spite of the ill-treatment it suffers at the hands, and mowing-machines, and vestries of man. His ideal of grass is growth that shall never be allowed to come to its flower and completion. He proves this in his lawns. Not only does he cut the coming grass-flower off by the stalk, but he does not allow the mere leaf—the blade—to perfect itself. He will not have it a "blade" at all; he cuts its top away as never sword or sabre was shaped. All the beauty of a blade of grass is that the organic shape has the intention of ending in a point. Surely no one at all aware of the beauty of lines ought to be ignorant of the significance and grace of manifest intention, which rules a living line from its beginning, even though the intention be towards a point while the first spring of the line is towards an opening curve. But man does not care for intention; he mows it. Nor does he care for attitude; he rolls it. In a word, he proves to the grass, as plainly as deeds can do so, that it is not to his mind. The rolling, especially, seems to be a violent way of showing that the universal grass interrupted by the life of the Englishman is not as he would have it. Besides, when he wishes to deride a city, he calls it grass-grown.

But his suburbs shall not, if he can help it, be grass-grown. They shall not be like a mere Pisa. Highgate shall not so, nor Peckham.

A WOMAN IN GREY

The mothers of Professors were indulged in the practice of jumping at conclusions, and were praised for their impatience of the slow process of reason.

Professors have written of the mental habits of women as though they accumulated generation by generation upon women, and passed over their sons. Professors take it for granted, obviously by some process other than the slow process of reason, that women derive from their mothers and grandmothers, and men from their fathers and grandfathers. This, for instance, was written lately: "This power [it matters not what] would be about equal in the two sexes but for the influence of heredity, which turns the scale in favour of the woman, as for long generations the surroundings and conditions of life of the female sex have developed in her a greater degree of the power in question than circumstances have required from men." "Long generations" of subjection are, strangely enough, held to excuse the timorousness and the shifts of women to-day. But the world, unknowing, tampers with the courage of its sons by such a slovenly indulgence. It tampers with their intelligence by fostering the ignorance of women.

And yet Shakespeare confessed the participation of man and woman in their common heritage. It is Cassius who speaks:

> "Have you not love enough to bear with me
> When that rash humour which my mother gave me
> Makes me forgetful?"

And Brutus who replies:

> "Yes, Cassius, and from henceforth
> When you are over-earnest with your Brutus
> He'll think your mother chides, and leave you so."

Dryden confessed it also in his praises of Anne Killigrew:

> "If by traduction came thy mind,
> Our wonder is the less to find
> A soul so charming from a stock so good.
> Thy father was transfused into thy blood."

The winning of Waterloo upon the Eton playgrounds is very well; but there have been some other, and happily minor, fields that were not won—that were more or less lost. Where did this loss take place, if the gains were secured at football? This inquiry is not quite so cheerful as the other. But while the victories were once going forward in the playground, the defeats or disasters were once going forward in some other place, presumably. And this was surely the place that was not a playground, the place where the future wives of the football players were sitting still while their future husbands were playing football.

This is the train of thought that followed the grey figure of a woman on a bicycle in Oxford Street. She had an enormous and top-heavy omnibus at her back. All the things on the near side of the street—the things going her way—were going at different paces, in two streams, overtaking and being overtaken. The tributary streets shot omnibuses and carriages, cabs and carts—some to go her own way, some with an impetus that carried them curving into the other current, and other some making a straight line right across Oxford Street into the street opposite. Besides all the unequal movement, there were the stoppings. It was a delicate tangle to keep from knotting. The nerves of the mouths of horses bore the whole charge and answered it, as they do every day.

The woman in grey, quite alone, was immediately dependent on no nerves but her own, which almost made her machine sensitive. But this alertness was joined to such perfect composure as no flutter of a moment disturbed. There was the steadiness of sleep, and a vigilance more than that of an ordinary waking.

At the same time, the woman was doing what nothing in her youth could well have prepared her for. She must have passed a childhood unlike the ordinary girl's childhood, if her steadiness or her alertness had ever been educated, if she had been rebuked for cowardice, for the egoistic distrust of general rules, or for claims of exceptional chances. Yet here she was, trusting not only herself but a multitude of other people; taking her equal risk; giving a watchful confidence to averages—that last, perhaps, her strangest and greatest success.

No exceptions were hers, no appeals, and no forewarnings. She evidently had not in her mind a single phrase, familiar to women, made to express no confidence except in accidents, and to proclaim a prudent foresight of the less probable event. No woman could ride a bicycle along Oxford Street with any such baggage as that about her.

The woman in grey had a watchful confidence not only in a multitude of men but in a multitude of things. And it is very hard for any untrained human being to practise confidence in things in motion—things full of force, and, what is worse, of forces. Moreover, there is a supreme difficulty for a mind accustomed to search timorously for some little place of insignificant rest on any accessible point of stable equilibrium; and that is the difficulty of holding itself nimbly secure in an equilibrium that is unstable. Who can deny that women are generally used to look about for the little stationary repose just described? Whether in intellectual or in spiritual things, they do not often live without it.

She, none the less, fled upon unstable equilibrium, escaped upon it, depended upon it, trusted it, was 'ware of it, was on guard against it, as she sped amid her crowd her own unstable equilibrium, her machine's, that of the judgment, the temper, the skill, the perception, the strength of men and horses.

She had learnt the difficult peace of suspense. She had learnt also the lowly and self-denying faith in common chances. She had learnt to be content with her share—no more—in common security, and to be pleased with her part in common hope. For all this, it may be repeated, she could have had but small preparation. Yet no anxiety was hers, no uneasy distrust and disbelief of that human thing—an average of life and death.

To this courage the woman in grey had attained with a spring, and she had seated herself suddenly upon a place of detachment between earth and air, freed from the principal detentions, weights, and embarrassments of the usual life of fear. She had made herself, as it were, light, so as not to dwell either in security or danger, but to pass between them. She confessed difficulty and peril by her delicate evasions, and consented to rest in neither. She would not owe safety to the mere motionlessness of a seat on the solid earth, but she used gravitation to balance the slight burdens of her wariness and her confidence. She put aside all the pride and vanity of terror, and leapt into an unsure condition of liberty and content.

She leapt, too, into a life of moments. No pause was possible to her as she went, except the vibrating pause of a perpetual change and of an unflagging flight. A woman, long educated to sit still, does not suddenly learn to live a momentary life without strong momentary resolution. She has no light achievement in limiting not only her foresight, which must become brief, but her memory, which must do more; for it must rather cease than become brief. Idle memory wastes time and other things. The moments of the woman in grey as they dropped by must needs disappear, and be simply forgotten, as a child forgets. Idle memory, by the way, shortens life, or shortens the sense of time, by linking the immediate past clingingly to the present. Here may possibly be found one of the reasons for the length of a child's time, and for the brevity of the time that succeeds. The child lets his moments pass by and quickly become remote through a thousand little successive oblivions. He has not yet the languid habit of recall.

"Thou art my warrior," said Volumnia. "I holp to frame thee."

Shall a man inherit his mother's trick of speaking, or her habit and attitude, and not suffer something, against his will, from her bequest of weakness, and something, against his heart, from her bequest of folly? From the legacies of an unlessoned mind, a woman's heirs-male are not cut off in the Common Law of the generations of mankind. Brutus knew that the valour of Portia was settled upon his sons.

SYMMETRY AND INCIDENT

The art of Japan has none but an exterior part in the history of the art of nations. Being in its own methods and attitude the art of accident, it has, appropriately, an accidental value. It is of accidental value, and not of integral necessity. The virtual discovery of Japanese art, during the later years of the second French Empire, caused Europe to relearn how expedient, how delicate, and how lovely Incident may look when Symmetry has grown vulgar. The lesson was most welcome. Japan has had her full influence. European art has learnt the value of position and the tact of the unique. But Japan is unlessoned, and (in all her characteristic art) content with her own conventions; she is local, provincial, alien, remote, incapable of equal companionship with a world that has Greek art in its own history—Pericles "to its father."

Nor is it pictorial art, or decorative art only, that has been touched by Japanese example of Incident and the Unique. Music had attained the noblest form of symmetry in the eighteenth century, but in music, too, symmetry had since grown dull; and momentary music, the music of phase and of fragment, succeeded. The sense of symmetry is strong in a complete melody—of symmetry in its most delicate and lively and least stationary form—balance; whereas the *leit-motif* is isolated. In domestic architecture Symmetry and Incident make a familiar antithesis—the very commonplace of rival methods of art. But the same antithesis exists in less obvious forms. The poets have sought "irregular" metres. Incident hovers, in the very act of choosing its right place, in the most modern of modern portraits. In these we have, if not the Japanese suppression of minor emphasis, certainly the Japanese exaggeration of major emphasis; and with this a quickness and buoyancy. The smile, the figure, the drapery—not yet settled from the arranging touch of a hand, and showing its mark—the restless and unstationary foot, and the unity of impulse that has passed everywhere like a single breeze, all these have a life that greatly transcends the life of Japanese art, yet has the nimble touch of Japanese incident. In passing, a charming comparison may be made between such portraiture and the aspect of an aspen or other tree of light and liberal leaf; whether still or in motion the aspen and the free-leafed poplar have the alertness and expectancy of flight in all their flocks of leaves, while the oaks and elms are gathered in their station. All this is not Japanese, but from such accident is Japanese art inspired, with its good luck of perceptiveness.

What symmetry is to form, that is repetition in the art of ornament. Greek art and Gothic alike have series, with repetition or counter-change for their ruling motive. It is hardly necessary to draw the distinction between this motive and that of the Japanese. The Japanese motives may be defined as uniqueness and position.

And these were not known as motives of decoration before the study of Japanese decoration. Repetition and counter-change, of course, have their place in Japanese ornament, as in the diaper patterns for which these people have so singular an invention, but here, too, uniqueness and position are the principal inspiration. And it is quite worth while, and much to the present purpose, to call attention to the chief peculiarity of the Japanese diaper patterns, which is *interruption*. Repetition there must necessarily be in these, but symmetry is avoided by an interruption which is, to the Western eye, at least, perpetually and freshly unexpected. The place of the interruptions of lines, the variation of the place, and the avoidance of correspondence, are precisely what makes Japanese design of this class inimitable. Thus, even in a repeating pattern, you have a curiously successful effect of impulse. It is as though a separate intention had been formed by the designer at every angle. Such renewed consciousness does not make for greatness. Greatness in design has more peace than is found in the gentle abruptness of Japanese lines, in their curious brevity. It is scarcely necessary to say that a line, in all other schools of art, is long or short according to its place and purpose; but only the Japanese designer so contrives his patterns that the line is always short; and many repeating designs are entirely composed of this various and variously-occurring brevity, this prankish avoidance of the goal. Moreover, the Japanese evade symmetry, in the unit of their repeating patterns, by another simple device—that of numbers. They make a small difference in the number of curves and of lines. A great difference would not make the same effect of variety; it would look too much like a contrast. For example, three rods on one side and six on another would be something else than a mere variation, and variety would be lost by the use of them. The Japanese decorator will vary three in this place by two in that, and a sense of the defeat of symmetry is immediately produced. With more violent means the idea of symmetry would have been neither suggested nor refuted.

Leaving mere repeating patterns and diaper designs, you find, in Japanese compositions, complete designs in which there is no point of symmetry. It is a balance of suspension and of antithesis. There is no sense of lack of equilibrium, because place is, most subtly, made to have the effect of giving or of subtracting value. A small thing is arranged to reply to a large one, for the small thing is placed at the precise distance that makes it a (Japanese) equivalent. In Italy (and perhaps in other countries) the scales commonly in use are furnished with only a single weight that increases or diminishes in value according as you slide it nearer or farther upon a horizontal arm. It is equivalent to so many ounces when it is close to the upright, and to so many pounds when it hangs from the farther end of the horizontal rod. Distance plays some such part with the twig or the bird in the upper corner of a Japanese composition. Its place is its significance and its value. Such an art of position implies a great art of intervals. The Japanese chooses a few things and leaves the space between them free, as free as the pauses or silences in music. But as time, not silence, is the subject, or material, of contrast in musical pauses, so it is the measurement of space—that is, collocation—that makes the value of empty intervals. The space between this form and that, in a Japanese composition, is valuable because it is just so wide and no more. And this, again, is only another way of saying that position is the principle of this apparently wilful art.

Moreover, the alien art of Japan, in its pictorial form, has helped to justify the more stenographic school of etching. Greatly transcending Japanese expression, the modern etcher has undoubtedly accepted moral support from the islands of the Japanese. He too etches a kind of shorthand, even though his notes appeal much to the spectator's knowledge, while the Oriental shorthand appeals to nothing but the spectator's simple vision. Thus the two artists work in ways dissimilar. Nevertheless, the French etcher would never have written his signs so freely had not the Japanese so freely drawn his own. Furthermore still, the transitory and destructible material of Japanese art has done as much as the multiplication of newspapers, and the discovery of processes, to reconcile the European designer—the black and white artist—to working for the day, the day of publication. Japan lives much of its daily life by means of paper, painted; so does Europe by means of paper, printed. But as we, unlike those Orientals, are a destructive people, paper with us means short life, quick abolition, transformation, re-appearance, a very circulation of life. This is our present way of surviving ourselves—the new version of that feat of life. Time was when to survive yourself meant to secure, for a time indefinitely longer than the life of man, such dull form as you had given to your work; to intrude upon posterity. To survive yourself, to-day, is to let your work go into daily oblivion.

Now, though the Japanese are not a destructive people, their paper does not last for ever, and that material has clearly suggested to them a different condition of ornament from that with which they adorned old lacquer, fine ivory, or other perdurable things. For the transitory material they keep the more purely pictorial art of landscape. What of Japanese landscape? Assuredly it is too far reduced to a monotonous convention to merit the serious study of races that have produced Cotman and Corot. Japanese landscape-drawing reduces things seen to such fewness as must have made the art insuperably tedious to any people less fresh-spirited and more inclined to take themselves seriously than these Orientals. A preoccupied people would never endure it. But a little closer attention from the Occidental student might find for their evasive attitude towards landscape—it is an attitude almost traitorously evasive—a more significant reason. It is that the distances, the greatness, the winds and the waves of the world, coloured plains, and the flight of a sky, are all certainly alien to the perceptions of a people intent upon little deformities. Does it seem harsh to define by that phrase the curious Japanese search for accidents? Upon such search these people are avowedly intent, even though they show themselves capable of exquisite appreciation of the form of a normal bird and of the habit of growth of a normal flower. They are not in search of the perpetual slight novelty which was Aristotle's ideal of the language poetic ("a little wildly, or with the flower of the mind," says Emerson of the way of a poet's speech)—and such novelty it is, like the frequent pulse of the pinion, that keeps verse upon the wing; no, what the Japanese are intent upon is perpetual slight disorder. In Japan the man in the fields has eyes less for the sky and the crescent moon than for some stone in the path, of which the asymmetry strikes his curious sense of pleasure in fortunate accident of form. For love of a little grotesque strangeness he will load himself with the stone and carry it home to his garden. The art of such a people is not liberal art, not the art of peace, and not the art of humanity. Look at the curls and curves whereby this people conventionally signify wave or cloud. All these curls have an attitude which is like that of a figure slightly malformed, and not like that of a human body that is perfect, dominant, and if bent, bent at no lowly or niggling labour. Why these curves should be so charming it would be hard to say; they have an exquisite prankishness of variety, the place where the upward or downward scrolls curl off from the main wave is delicately unexpected every time, and—especially in gold embroideries—is sensitively fit for the material, catching and losing the light, while the lengths of waving line are such as the long gold threads take by nature.

A moment ago this art was declared not human. And, in fact, in no other art has the figure suffered such crooked handling. The Japanese have generally evaded even the local beauty of their own race for the sake of perpetual slight deformity. Their beauty is remote from our sympathy and admiration; and it is quite possible that we might miss it in pictorial presentation, and that the Japanese artist may have intended human beauty where we do not recognise it. But if it is not easy to recognise, it is certainly not difficult to guess at. And, accordingly, you are generally aware that the separate beauty of the race, and its separate dignity, even—to be very generous—has been admired by the Japanese artist, and is represented here and there occasionally, in the figure of warrior or mousmé. But even with this exception the habit of Japanese figure-drawing is evidently grotesque, derisive, and crooked. It is curious to observe that the search for slight deformity is so constant as to make use, for its purposes, not of action only, but of perspective foreshortening. With us it is to the youngest child only that there would appear to be mirth in the drawing of a man who, stooping violently forward, would seem to have his head "beneath his shoulders." The European child would not see fun in the living man so presented, but—unused to the same effect "in the flat"—he thinks it prodigiously humorous in a drawing. But so only when he is quite young. The Japanese keeps, apparently, his sense of this kind of humour. It amuses him, but not perhaps altogether as it amuses the child, that the foreshortened figure should, in drawing and to the unpractised eye, seem distorted and dislocated; the simple Oriental appears to find more derision in it than the simple child. The distortion is not without a suggestion of ignominy. And, moreover, the Japanese shows derision, but not precisely scorn. He does not hold himself superior to his hideous models. He makes free with them on equal terms. He is familiar with them.

And if this is the conviction gathered from ordinary drawings, no need to insist upon the ignoble character of those that are intentional caricatures.

Perhaps the time has hardly come for writing anew the praises of symmetry. The world knows too much of the abuse of Greek decoration, and would be glad to forget it, with the intention of learning that art afresh in a future age and of seeing it then anew. But whatever may be the phases of the arts, there is the abiding principle of symmetry in the body of man, that goes erect, like an upright soul. Its balance is equal. Exterior human symmetry is surely a curious physiological fact where there is no symmetry interiorly. For the centres of life and movement within the body are placed with Oriental inequality. Man is Greek without and Japanese within. But the absolute symmetry of the skeleton and of the beauty and life that cover it is accurately a principle. It controls, but not tyrannously, all the life of human action. Attitude and motion disturb perpetually, with infinite incidents— inequalities of work, war, and pastime, inequalities of sleep—the symmetry of man. Only in death and "at attention" is that symmetry complete in attitude. Nevertheless, it rules the dance and the battle, and its rhythm is not to be destroyed. All the more because this hand holds the goad and that the harrow, this the shield and that the sword, because this hand rocks the cradle and that caresses the unequal heads of children, is this rhythm the law; and grace and strength are inflections thereof. All human movement is a variation upon symmetry, and without symmetry it would not be variation; it would be lawless, fortuitous, and as dull and broadcast as lawless art. The order of inflection that is not infraction has been explained in a most authoritative sentence of criticism of literature, a sentence that should save the world the trouble of some of its futile, violent, and weak experiments: "Law, the rectitude of humanity," says Mr Coventry Patmore, "should be the poet's only subject, as, from time immemorial, it has been the subject of true art, though many a true artist has done the Muse's will and knew it not. As all the music of verse arises, not from infraction but from inflection of the law of the set metre; so the greatest poets have been those the *modulus* of whose verse has been most variously and delicately inflected, in correspondence with feelings and passions which are the inflections of moral law in their theme. Law puts a strain upon feeling, and feeling responds with a strain upon law. Furthermore, Aristotle says that the quality of poetic language is a continual *slight* novelty. In the highest poetry, like that of Milton, these three modes of inflection, metrical, linguistical, and moral, all chime together in praise of the truer order of life."

And like that order is the order of the figure of man, an order most beautiful and most secure when it is put to the proof. That perpetual proof by perpetual inflection is the very condition of life. Symmetry is a profound, if disregarded because perpetually inflected, condition of human life.

The nimble art of Japan is unessential; it may come and go, may settle or be fanned away. It has life and it is not without law; it has an obvious life, and a less obvious law. But with Greece abides the obvious law and the less obvious life: symmetry as apparent as the symmetry of the form of man, and life occult like his unequal heart. And this seems to be the nobler and the more perdurable relation.

THE ILLUSION OF HISTORIC TIME

He who has survived his childhood intelligently must become conscious of something more than a change in his sense of the present and in his apprehension of the future. He must be aware of no less a thing than the destruction of the past. Its events and empires stand where they did, and the mere relation of time is as it was. But that which has fallen together, has fallen in, has fallen close, and lies in a little heap, is the past itself—time—the fact of antiquity.

He has grown into a smaller world as he has grown older. There are no more extremities. Recorded time has no more terrors. The unit of measure which he holds in his hand has become in his eyes a thing of paltry length. The discovery draws in the annals of mankind. He had thought them to be wide.

For a man has nothing whereby to order and place the floods, the states, the conquests, and the temples of the past, except only the measure which he holds. Call that measure a space of ten years. His first ten years had given him the illusion of a most august scale and measure. It was then that he conceived Antiquity. But now! Is it to a decade of ten such little years as these now in his hand—ten of his mature years—that men give the dignity of a century? They call it an age; but what if life shows now so small that the word age has lost its gravity?

In fact, when a child begins to know that there is a past, he has a most noble rod to measure it by—he has his own ten years. He attributes an overwhelming majesty to all recorded time. He confers distance. He, and he alone, bestows mystery. Remoteness is his. He creates more than mortal centuries. He sends armies fighting into the extremities of the past. He assigns the Parthenon to a hill of ages, and the temples of Upper Egypt to sidereal time.

If there were no child, there would be nothing old. He, having conceived old time, communicates a remembrance at least of the mystery to the mind of the man. The man perceives at last all the illusion, but he cannot forget what was his conviction when he was a child. He had once a persuasion of Antiquity. And this is not for nothing. The enormous undeception that comes upon him still leaves spaces in his mind.

But the undeception is rude work. The man receives successive shocks. It is as though one strained level eyes towards the horizon, and then were bidden to shorten his sight and to close his search within a poor half acre before his face. Now, it is that he suddenly perceives the hitherto remote, remote youth of his own parents to have been something familiarly near, so measured by his new standard; again, it is the coming of Attila that is displaced. Those ten last years of his have corrected the world. There needs no other rod than that ten years' rod to chastise all the imaginations of the spirit of man. It makes history skip.

To have lived through any appreciable part of any century is to hold thenceforth a mere century cheap enough. But, it may be said, the mystery of change remains. Nay, it does not. Change that trudges through our own world—our contemporary world—is not very mysterious. We perceive its pace; it is a jog-trot. Even so, we now consider, jolted the changes of the past, with the same hurry.

The man, therefore, who has intelligently ceased to be a child scans through a shortened avenue the reaches of the past. He marvels that he was so deceived. For it was a very deception. If the Argonauts, for instance, had been children, it would have been well enough for the child to measure their remoteness and their acts with his own magnificent measure. But they were only men and demi-gods. Thus they belong to him as he is now—a man; and not to him as he was once—a child. It was quite wrong to lay the child's enormous ten years' rule along the path from our time to theirs; that path must be skipped by the nimble yard in the man's present possession. Decidedly the Argonauts are no subject for the boy.

What, then? Is the record of the race nothing but a bundle of such little times? Nay, it seems that childhood, which created the illusion of ages, does actually prove it true. Childhood is itself Antiquity—to every man his only Antiquity. The recollection of childhood cannot make Abraham old again in the mind of a man of thirty-five; but the beginning of every life is older than Abraham. *There* is the abyss of time. Let a man turn to his own childhood—no further—if he would renew his sense of remoteness, and of the mystery of change.

For in childhood change does not go at that mere hasty amble; it rushes; but it has enormous space for its flight. The child has an apprehension not only of things far off, but of things far apart; an illusive apprehension when he is learning "ancient" history—a real apprehension when he is conning his own immeasurable infancy. If there is no historical Antiquity worth speaking of, this is the renewed and unnumbered Antiquity for all mankind.

And it is of this—merely of this—that "ancient" history seems to partake. Rome was founded when we began Roman history, and that is why it seems long ago. Suppose the man of thirty-five heard, at that present age, for the first time of Romulus. Why, Romulus would be nowhere. But he built his wall, as a matter of fact, when every one was seven years old. It is by good fortune that "ancient" history is taught in the only ancient days. So, for a time, the world is magical.

Modern history does well enough for learning later. But by learning something of antiquity in the first ten years, the child enlarges the sense of time for all mankind. For even after the great illusion is over and history is re-measured, and all fancy and flight caught back and chastised, the enlarged sense remains enlarged. The man remains capable of great spaces of time. He will not find them in Egypt, it is true, but he finds them within, he contains them, he is aware of them. History has fallen together, but childhood surrounds and encompasses history, stretches beyond and passes on the road to eternity.

He has not passed in vain through the long ten years, the ten years that are the treasury of preceptions—the first. The great disillusion shall never shorten those years, nor set nearer together the days that made them. "Far apart," I have said, and that "far apart" is wonderful. The past of childhood is not single, is not motionless, nor fixed in one point; it has summits a world away one from the other. Year from year differs as the antiquity of Mexico from the antiquity of Chaldea. And the man of thirty-five knows for ever afterwards what is flight, even though he finds no great historic distances to prove his wings by.

There is a long and mysterious moment in long and mysterious childhood, which is the extremest distance known to any human fancy. Many other moments, many other hours, are long in the first ten years. Hours of weariness are long—not with a mysterious length, but with a mere length of protraction, so that the things called minutes and half-hours by the elderly may be something else to their apparent contemporaries, the children. The ancient moment is not merely one of these—it is a space not of long, but of immeasurable, time. It is the moment of going to sleep. The man knows that borderland, and has a contempt for it: he has long ceased to find antiquity there. It has become a common enough margin of dreams to him; and he does not attend to its phantasies. He knows that he has a frolic spirit in his head which has its way at those hours, but he is not interested in it. It is the inexperienced child who passes with simplicity through the marginal country; and the thing he meets there is principally the yet further conception of illimitable time.

His nurse's lullaby is translated into the mysteries of time. She sings absolutely immemorial words. It matters little what they may mean to waking ears; to the ears of a child going to sleep they tell of the beginning of the world. He has fallen asleep to the sound of them all his life; and "all his life" means more than older speech can well express.

Ancient custom is formed in a single spacious year. A child is beset with long traditions. And his infancy is so old, so old, that the mere adding of years in the life to follow will not seem to throw it further back—it is already so far. That is, it looks as remote to the memory of a man of thirty as to that of a man of seventy. What are a mere forty years of added later life in the contemplation of such a distance? Pshaw!

EYES

There is nothing described with so little attention, with such slovenliness, or so without verification—albeit with so much confidence and word-painting—as the eyes of the men and women whose faces have been made memorable by their works. The describer generally takes the first colour that seems to him probable. The grey eyes of Coleridge are recorded in a proverbial line, and Procter repeats the word, in describing from the life. Then Carlyle, who shows more signs of actual attention, and who caught a trick of Coleridge's pronunciation instantly, proving that with his hearing at least he was not slovenly, says that Coleridge's eyes were brown—"strange, brown, timid, yet earnest-looking eyes." A Coleridge with brown eyes is one man, and a Coleridge with grey eyes another—and, as it were, more responsible. As to Rossetti's eyes, the various inattention of his friends has assigned to them, in all the ready-made phrases, nearly all the colours.

So with Charlotte Brontë. Matthew Arnold seems to have thought the most probable thing to be said of her eyes was that they were grey and expressive. Thus, after seeing them, does he describe them in one of his letters. Whereas Mrs Gaskell, who shows signs of attention, says that Charlotte's eyes were a reddish hazel, made up of "a great variety of tints," to be discovered by close looking. Almost all eyes that are not brown are, in fact, of some such mixed colour, generally spotted in, and the effect is vivacious. All the more if the speckled iris has a dark ring to enclose it.

Nevertheless, the eye of mixed colour has always a definite character, and the mingling that looks green is quite unlike the mingling that looks grey; and among the greys there is endless difference. Brown eyes alone are apart, unlike all others, but having no variety except in the degrees of their darkness.

The colour of eyes seems to be significant of temperament, but as regards beauty there is little or nothing to choose among colours. It is not the eye, but the eyelid, that is important, beautiful, eloquent, full of secrets. The eye has nothing but its colour, and all colours are fine within fine eyelids. The eyelid has all the form, all the drawing, all the breadth and length; the square of great eyes irregularly wide; the long corners of narrow eyes; the pathetic outward droop; the delicate contrary suggestion of an upward turn at the outer corner, which Sir Joshua loved.

It is the blood that is eloquent, and there is no sign of blood in the eye; but in the eyelid the blood hides itself and shows its signs. All along its edges are the little muscles, living, that speak not only the obvious and emphatic things, but what reluctances, what perceptions, what ambiguities, what half-apprehensions, what doubts, what interceptions! The eyelids confess, and reject, and refuse to reject.

They have expressed all things ever since man was man.

And they express so much by seeming to hide or to reveal that which indeed expresses nothing. For there is no message from the eye. It has direction, it moves, in the service of the sense of sight; it receives the messages of the world. But expression is outward, and the eye has it not. There are no windows of the soul, there are only curtains; and these show all things by seeming to hide a little more, a little less. They hide nothing but their own secrets.

But, some may say, the eyes have emotion inasmuch as they betray it by the waxing and contracting of the pupils. It is, however, the rarest thing, this opening and narrowing under any influences except those of darkness and light. It does take place exceptionally; but I am doubtful whether those who talk of it have ever really been attentive enough to perceive it. A nervous woman, brown-eyed and young, who stood to tell the news of her own betrothal, and kept her manners exceedingly composed as she spoke, had this waxing and closing of the pupils; it went on all the time like a slow, slow pulse. But such a thing is not to be seen once a year.

Moreover, it is—though so significant—hardly to be called expression. It is not articulate. It implies emotion, but does not define, or describe, or divide it. It is touching, insomuch as we have knowledge of the perturbed tide of the spirit that must cause it, but it is not otherwise eloquent. It does not tell us the quality of the thought, it does not inform and surprise as with intricacies. It speaks no more explicit or delicate things than does the pulse in its quickening. It speaks with less division of meanings than does the taking of the breath, which has impulses and degrees.

No, the eyes do their work, but do it blankly, without communication. Openings into the being they may be, but the closed cheek is more communicative. From them the blood of Perdita never did look out. It ebbed and flowed in her face, her dance, her talk. It was hiding in her paleness, and cloistered in her reserve, but visible in prison. It leapt and looked, at a word. It was conscious in the fingers that reached out flowers. It ran with her. It was silenced when she hushed her answers to the king. Everywhere it was close behind the doors—everywhere but in her eyes.

How near at hand was it, then, in the living eyelids that expressed her in their minute and instant and candid manner! All her withdrawals, every hesitation, fluttered there. A flock of meanings and intelligences alighted on those mobile edges.

Think, then, of all the famous eyes in the world, that said so much, and said it in no other way but only by the little exquisite muscles of their lids. How were these ever strong enough to bear the burden of those eyes of Heathcliff's in "Wuthering Heights"? "The clouded windows of Hell flashed a moment towards me; the fiend which usually looked out, however, was so dimmed and drowned—" That mourning fiend, who had wept all night, had no expression, no proof or sign of himself, except in the edges of the eyelids of the man.

And the eyes of Garrick? Eyelids, again. And the eyes of Charles Dickens, that were said to contain the life of fifty men? On the mechanism of the eyelids hung that fifty-fold vitality. "Bacon had a delicate, lively, hazel eye," says Aubrey in his "Lives of Eminent Persons." But nothing of this belongs to the eye except the colour. Mere brightness the eyeball has or has not, but so have many glass beads: the liveliness is the eyelid's. "Dr Harvey told me it was like the eie of a viper." So intent and narrowed must have been the attitude of Bacon's eyelids.

"I never saw such another eye in a human, head," says Scott in describing Burns, "though I have seen the most distinguished men in my time. It was large, and of a dark cast, and glowed (I say literally glowed) when he spoke with feeling or interest. The eye alone, I think, indicated the poetical character and temperament." No eye literally glows; but some eyes are polished a little more, and reflect. And this is the utmost that can possibly have been true as to the eyes of Burns. But set within the meanings of impetuous eyelids the lucidity of the dark eyes seemed broken, moved, directed into fiery shafts.

See, too, the reproach of little, sharp, grey eyes addressed to Hazlitt. There are neither large nor small eyes, say physiologists, or the difference is so small as to be negligeable. But in the eyelids the difference is great between large and small, and also between the varieties of largeness. Some have large openings, and some are in themselves broad and long, serenely covering eyes called small. Some have far more drawing than others, and interesting foreshortenings and sweeping curves.

Where else is spirit so evident? And where else is it so spoilt? There is no vulgarity like the vulgarity of vulgar eyelids. They have a slang all their own, of an intolerable kind. And eyelids have looked all the cruel looks that have ever made wounds in innocent souls meeting them surprised.

But all love and all genius have winged their flight from those slight and unmeasurable movements, have flickered on the margins of lovely eyelids quick with thought. Life, spirit, sweetness are there in a small place; using the finest and the slenderest machinery; expressing meanings a whole world apart, by a difference of material action so fine that the sight which appreciates it cannot detect it; expressing intricacies of intellect; so incarnate in slender and sensitive flesh that nowhere else in the body of man is flesh so spiritual.

Lector House believes that a society develops through a two-fold approach of continuous learning and adaptation, which is derived from the study of classic literary works spread across the historic timeline of literature records. Therefore, we aim at reviving, repairing and redeveloping all those inaccessible or damaged but historically as well as culturally important literature across subjects so that the future generations may have an opportunity to study and learn from past works to embark upon a journey of creating a better future.

This book is a result of an effort made by Lector House towards making a contribution to the preservation and repair of original ancient works which might hold historical significance to the approach of continuous learning across subjects.

HAPPY READING & LEARNING!

LECTOR HOUSE LLP
E-MAIL: lectorpublishing@gmail.com